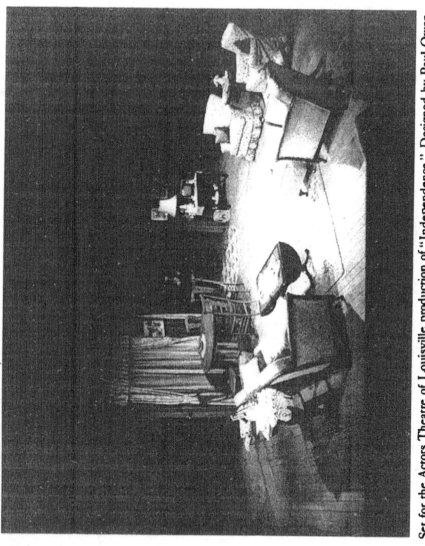

Set for the Actors Theatre of Louisville production of "Independence." Designed by Paul Owen.

INDEPENDENCE

A PLAY IN TWO ACTS BY
LEE BLESSING

★

★

DRAMATISTS
PLAY SERVICE
INC.

2

To Jeanne Blake,
the Eugene O'Neill
Theater Center
and Actors Theatre of Louisville.

INDEPENDENCE was given its professional premiere by the Actors Theatre of Louisville during its Eighth Annual Humana Festival of New American Plays in February, 1984. It was directed by Patrick Tovatt; the scenery was designed by Paul Owen; the costumes were designed by Geoffrey T. Cunningham; and the sound design was by James M. Bay. The cast was as follows:

JO .... Shelley Crandall

KESS................................. Deborah Hedwall

SHERRY............................... Gretchen West

EVELYN............................... Sylvia Gassell

INDEPENDENCE was developed in workshop at the Cricket Theatre in Minneapolis, Minnesota.

INDEPENDENCE was initially presented as a staged reading at the Eugene O'Neill Theater Center's 1983 National Playwrights Conference.

CHARACTERS

TIME

Late May. The present.

PLACE

Independence, Iowa.

ACT ONE

ACT TWO

INDEPENDENCE

ACT ONE
Scene One

Interior of an old frame house. Downstage is the living room, Upstage is the front porch. The effect should be of a dark room in the foreground, backed by the bright afternoon sunlight coming through the porch. Right is a door to Sherry's room. Left, a door to the kitchen. Up Right, a hallway leads upstairs. Up Left, an archway leading to the dining room. The living room is filled with old-fashioned furniture: a couch, overstuffed chairs, etc. Well kept up.

After a moment, Jo comes through the screen door, onto the porch. She wears an orthopedic collar. Kess follows, carrying a travel bag.

JO. I can't believe it! You look incredible, you're so tan. How do you get so tan in Minneapolis?
KESS. Jo, shouldn't you be lying down?
JO. Oh, I'm fine. Here, let me take your bag...
KESS. That's ok. I've got it...
JO. *(Entering the living room.)* Well, come on in. Take a look at the old place. What do you think? After four years.
KESS. *(Remaining on the threshold.)* I think you should be lying down.
JO. Don't worry. This is my last day to wear this. The doctor said I'm fine if I don't move fast.
KESS. On the phone you said it was an emergency.
JO. It is an emergency.

7

KESS. You said you were laid up. I came down because I thought you couldn't get out of bed.

JO. I have been laid up. It's just that...

KESS. What do you mean? You're waltzing all over the room. If you've only got a minor injury...

JO. I broke my neck. Well... I chipped it. One of those little bones back there. The doctor said I could have been paralyzed for life. Really. I could have died. *(Of the collar.)* I've had to wear this for a week, I strained the muscles so bad.

KESS. You made me leave my work — you made me drive for hours — because you chipped your neck?

JO. Well ... yes.

KESS. Why?

JO. Are you going to come in or not? *(Kess turns to go.)* Kess! That's not funny. *(Kess stops, looks at her.)* Please come in. *(Kess enters, stands uncomfortably in the room.)*

KESS. How'd you get hurt? *(A beat. Kess turns again for the door.)*

JO. Someone tried to kill me.

KESS. Kill you? Who?

JO. Mom.

KESS. Mom tried to...? Why didn't you tell me on the phone?

JO. I couldn't say it over the phone...

KESS. She tried to *kill* you?

JO. Well, yes... in a way. She hit me. And I fell. I fell six feet. Into the street. You know — over by Duman's Drug? Where the street goes down? It's a six-foot drop from the sidewalk, and ... she pushed me.

KESS. You said she hit you.

JO. She did hit me, but it was like a push. I mean, I fell over backwards. On my neck. I was almost hit by a Plymouth. I didn't wake up for a couple of minutes.

KESS. Did they see it? The person in the Plymouth?

JO. No, they were coming around the corner.

KESS. Did anybody see it?

JO. No, it was Sunday. The stores were closed. But it

8

happened.

KESS. Why would Mom hit you?

JO. Because I'm pregnant. *(A beat.)* How do you like the house? We painted it last year. *(Kess moves to a chair, puts down her bag, but remains standing.)*

KESS. It's great to be home. I can only stay a couple days. I'm teaching three different courses...

JO. I don't expect you to stay long — honest. I just need you to be here awhile, for support. I need help with Mom, and ... things. You know Mom.

KESS. Yes, I know Mom.

JO. I need you to ... stand up to her. You know — like last time.

KESS. Last time I committed her for three months. Is that what you're talking about?

JO. Oh, no — no, no, no, no, no, no. No. I don't mean that. I just mean having you back would ... help so much. You know, having *all* her daughters here for once, for her to...

KESS. Contend with.

JO. *No*, to ... love. *(Sherry enters from her room with a makeup kit.)*

SHERRY. Hey, is that big sister?

JO. Sherry — thought you were taking a shower.

SHERRY. I will tomorrow. *(Setting up a mirror, taking her brush out of the kit.)* Hi, Kess. How're you? Hope you don't mind if I do this while I say hello. I have to go to work. Nice to see you. *(She begins doing her makeup.)*

KESS. Nice to see you.

SHERRY. How you been the last four years?

KESS. Fine. You?

SHERRY. I'm getting out of school in a couple weeks. At long last. Would you believe it?

KESS. You look different.

SHERRY. I hope so. Christ, I was 15 the last time you saw me. You just here for the day?

KESS. Well...

9

SHERRY. Stay long enough to catch Mom's act. She's really been lighting up the place lately. Ever since Jo got knocked up. Same routine as with me. Something about unmarried pregnant daughters just rings her bell. Check her out. She'll be back from work in a little while.

JO. *(Moving toward the kitchen.)* Kess, why don't we...

KESS. I didn't know she worked.

SHERRY. *(Laughs.)* Oh, yeah. She volunteers out at the MHI.

KESS. Since when?

SHERRY. Almost a year. Jo got her the job. Didn't you write her about that, Jo? Mom's like this model volunteer out there. She made the local paper and everything. "Former Mental Patient Now Helps Others At Mental Health Institute." You know, one of those articles that makes you feel ten feet tall 'n shit? *Look* at this hair of mine. I gotta work tonight.

KESS. *(To Jo.)* Mom's working with mental patients?

SHERRY. Don't worry. She won't hurt 'em. She's just in the craft center. They don't let her alone with anybody.

JO. She wanted to. I couldn't say no.

SHERRY. Hey, what do you think of the pregnant one here? She tell you all about it?

KESS. Not yet.

SHERRY. It's really ridiculous, believe me. I'm sorry, Jo, but it is. I mean, imagine this: Jo, who's been a virgin practically since pioneer days, finally decided to go out with someone. Did she write you about that? So guess what? She goes out with him and goes out with him. And in the course of human events, she gets pregnant.

JO. His name is Don Orbeck.

SHERRY. Deadeye Don Orbeck.

KESS. *(To Jo.)* Well, what's he like?

SHERRY. He's got a Subaru — that's about it. So anyhow, he offers to marry Jo...

KESS. He wants to marry you?

SHERRY. *Did* want to. Jo said no.

10

KESS. You didn't want to marry him?

SHERRY. She turned him down.

JO. It would have been selfish. *(They look at her.)* To marry him and leave Mom all alone? He's not going to live with her, you know.

SHERRY. He's not completely stupid.

JO. Besides, I think he was just ... offering. You know, 'cause he felt he had to. *(Sherry has pulled hair out of her brush and thrown it on the floor. Kess bends to pick it up.)*

SHERRY. What are you doing?

KESS. Just...

SHERRY. Are you picking up after me?

KESS. You threw hair on the floor.

SHERRY. Put it back. *(Kess hesitates, then does so.)* I *have* a mother for that. So, anyway— like I say, now Jo's alone and pregnant, and there's this marksman walking around town, beginning to look for other targets.

JO. Sherry.

SHERRY. Well, he is. You know who he's showing up at Popeye's with now?

JO. Who?

SHERRY. You want to go insane? Heidi Joy Duckly.

JO. You're kidding.

SHERRY. Nope. Heidi Joy. *(To Kess.)* She's this blonde dwarf you wouldn't believe. I mean, Don was never too inventive, but *Heidi.* You know what Heidi once said to me out loud? "Women should never complain — that's the man's job." Really. I could've strangled the bitch. *(Kess has by now walked up to the front windows, and looks out.)* So what do you think of Jo's life? Screwed up, huh? And I thought I was in trouble when *I* had a kid...

JO. *(To Sherry.)* You should have let me tell her about Don.

SHERRY. You would've taken all day. Hey, Kess. You like my hair this way?

KESS. What? Oh ... sure.

SHERRY. You're not even looking. What are you looking at?

KESS. The traffic light.

11

SHERRY. *The* traffic light. That's about it. Independence, Iowa.

KESS. Same houses. Even the same billboards.

SHERRY. Only so many ways to sell herbicide. I'll be out of here so fast when I graduate. I'm 19 years old and still in high school. That's the real cost of illegitimate kids, believe me. Jo, you were smart to wait.

KESS. I can see the MHI from here.

SHERRY. Second home to the demented of northeast Iowa. And I do mean Mom and Jo.

JO. Sherry...

SHERRY. *(Rising, after packing up her kit.)* I don't mean it. Just that anybody who works out there is bound to bring some of it home with her.

JO. I work in accounts. I never go near the patients.

KESS. *(Looking off to the side.)* Mrs. Anderberg's collection has grown.

SHERRY. Yeah. Lawn Ornament Land. She must have twenty of 'em out there. All the Iowa standards: stable boys, little fawns, sleeping Mexicans... Hey! You know what? I could use those in a sculpture, I bet. You know — just mush 'em all together some way? Shit, what a great idea. I wonder if I could buy some of them off her tomorrow? I'm an artist.

KESS. Oh? That's nice.

SHERRY. No, really. I won a thing at school. I'm a killer. Even my teacher thinks so.

KESS. That's excellent. I'm impressed.

SHERRY. "That's excellent. I'm impressed." Same old Kess.

JO. Sherry, aren't you late for work?

SHERRY. Don't you wish. Mom and Jo are officially ashamed of me, now that I'm a barmaid at Popeye's.

KESS. Popeye's? Doesn't the school get mad?

SHERRY. Nah. They're too desperate to get rid of me. I graduate in three weeks. *(Taking her kit into her room.)* Hey, how do you like this? I moved downstairs. It's not exactly a separate apartment, but almost. I still think my big mistake was not getting a separate apartment at birth.

KESS. Sherry?

SHERRY. *(Off.)* What?

KESS. How do you think Mom's doing?

SHERRY. *(Returning with a light jacket.)* Oh, fine. Never better. Last night she threw her shoe at my boyfriend. We were sitting in the den, watching tv. Mom was in there, sewing. Me and this guy were hugging and shit — nothing special. Suddenly she chucked her loafer at him. Then she went back to sewing, no explanation. She's great.

KESS. How did Jo get hurt?

JO. I told you...

SHERRY. Mom shoved her off the sidewalk or something, I don't know. Something lame like that. Hey, I gotta go work. Popeye's is sleazy, but it's all money. *(She moves toward the front door.)* Tell me about yourself sometime. See you later. 'Night. *(Stops again.)* This place seem any different to you?

KESS. Yes. A little.

SHERRY. It's not. *(She exits out the front door.)*

KESS. Well. She sure hasn't changed, has she?

JO. Not much. *(Jo picks up the hair on the floor, disposes of it.)*

KESS. So. Mom is not happy.

JO. She's been terrible. Even after I told her I wasn't going to marry Don — that I was going to stay here. She acts like she doesn't believe me.

KESS. Do you think about leaving her?

JO. I couldn't leave her.

KESS. I did.

JO. You're you. You could do that.

KESS. Everyone does that. People grow up. They leave home. *(During Jo's next speech, Evelyn appears unnoticed in the dining room. She wears a coat. She stops when she sees Kess.)*

JO. They don't leave homes like this one. Mom needs more help than other people. She needs someone to be here. Steadily.

KESS. You, you mean?

JO. Well, yes me. If no one else is going to do it. *(A beat.)* I'm sorry.

13

She still hasn't forgiven you, you know.

EVELYN. *(Moving into the living room.)* Who says I haven't forgiven her?

JO. Mom!

EVELYN. It's silly to say that I haven't forgiven Kess. Where did you get that idea?

JO. Well ... you said...

EVELYN. *(Coming to Kess.)* I can't tell you how surprised I felt when Jo told me you were coming. I hope you'll feel comfortable here.

KESS. Thanks.

EVELYN. Do you want some tea?

KESS. No, thanks.

EVELYN. No? Coffee? Anything?

KESS. No.

EVELYN. Well, I'd like some tea. Jo, why don't you be good and make us some, all right? The way we like it?

JO. Oh ... um, ok. *(She exits to the kitchen.)*

EVELYN. Have a seat.

KESS. In a minute.

EVELYN. *(Sitting near Kess's bag.)* I will. I've been standing for hours. Out at the MHI. I work in the craft center, you know.

KESS. I heard.

EVELYN. I thought you'd be interested, since you were the one who brought me out there in the first place. Of course, now I'm helping other people, instead of being helped. They all like the projects I think up. Just simple things, really. Wood and yarn and paint and things. *(Evelyn opens Kess's bag and rummages inside.)* How long are you staying? Did you bring a lot with you?

KESS. What are you doing?

EVELYN. Looking at your things. *(Holding up a book.)* What's this book? It's awfully thick.

KESS. It's a study of imagery in 17th-Century Scottish Border Ballads.

EVELYN. What do you use it for? Do you read it?

KESS. I'm writing a book of my own.

14

EVELYN. Really? What's your book called?

KESS. "Imagery in 17th-Century Scottish Border Ballads."

EVELYN. Isn't that the same thing?

KESS. It's my view.

EVELYN. *(Laughs, continues rummaging.)* I'll never understand it.

KESS. Mom, why are you going through my things?

EVELYN. I haven't seen you. I'm trying to get an idea of who you are. How you've changed, I mean.

KESS. *(Retrieving her bag, moving it away from her.)* I haven't.

EVELYN. You came back. How long are you staying?

KESS. Jo and I are still talking that one over.

EVELYN. I hope you stay a long time. It's exciting to have all you girls together again. It's a rare treat.

KESS. Jo said you tried to kill her.

EVELYN. Why don't you sit down?

KESS. I'll sit down when I want to sit down.

EVELYN. Are you afraid to sit down? *(A beat. Kess sits in a chair.)* You always used to sit there. *(Kess immediately rises.)* It's so hard to know what to start talking about after four years, isn't it? Are you still a homosexual?

KESS. *(A beat.)* Yes, Mother. I am still a homosexual.

EVELYN. I suppose that'll make it hard for you to give Jo much advice about this Don Orbeck fellow. She's awfully confused right now. She wanted to marry him, but I think I've pointed out the disadvantages of *that*.

KESS. What are they?

EVELYN. Oh — well, everyone counsels against getting married because of an inadvertant pregnancy. I mean, look at my own life. I married Henry Briggs just because we were expecting you, and that didn't work out so wonderfully, did it?

KESS. I guess not.

EVELYN. What is it about the women in this family? We get near a man, and the next thing we know we're pregnant. You're probably right to stay away from men.

KESS. Mom...

15

EVELYN. Are you sure you don't want to sit? I feel like I'm staring up at a big building.

KESS. I'll stand.

EVELYN. I hope you won't do any homosexual things while you're in town. I mean, it's your life, but...

KESS. *(Moving toward the kitchen.)* I wonder if Jo needs help?

EVELYN. Oh, she's gone down to the bakery for some rolls.

KESS. She has?

EVELYN. She always does when she makes tea. It's one of our little sins.

KESS. *(Sighs, perches on the back of a chair.)* Oh.

EVELYN. It's been so long since we've talked. I admit, I wished you dead there for a couple of years, but I'm over that now.

KESS. Mom...

EVELYN. Jo's almost fully recovered, too. From her neck, I mean. So, I guess you'd say we're all doing very well at the...

KESS. Mom, can I say something?

EVELYN. Of course. We're having a talk.

KESS. As I was driving down here, I was talking to myself — I was saying, "Mom's had four years. We both have. Four years of not seeing each other, not talking, not even writing. Maybe things are entirely different by now. Maybe we'll actually find that we've forgotten how we used to talk to each other. Maybe we'll invent a whole new way."

EVELYN. You talk to yourself in the car?

KESS. Why do we get into conversations like this?! Can't you just say, "Hello, Kess — it's nice to see you again"?

EVELYN. No.

KESS. Why not?

EVELYN. Because it isn't.

KESS. *(A beat.)* Why not?

EVELYN. Isn't it obvious? You left this family long ago. You never visited, you never told us anything about your life...

KESS. I was trying to establish something for myself.

EVELYN. And then, four years ago, out of the blue, you came down here and decided I needed medical help.

16

KESS. You did.

EVELYN. In your opinion.

KESS. I found you sitting on the floor behind a chair, wrapped in a blanket.

EVELYN. And you gave me a hug. I remember; it was very sweet. Then you took me out to the MHI, and...

KESS. What did you want me to do? Take you up to Minneapolis with me? You wouldn't go. Quit my job? Move down here?

EVELYN. That could have been a start.

KESS. I'm a professional! I have a career. It takes all my time and energy — all my love to do it well. I'm not a hack teacher somewhere. I'm extremely good at what I do.

EVELYN. I know, dear. You're a specialist.

KESS. You were only in there three months.

EVELYN. How much love would you like, Kess?

KESS. What?

EVELYN. Isn't that what we're talking about? Really? You're not here for Jo. You're here for love. You want some of my love.

KESS. That would be nice.

EVELYN. Well then, it occurs to me we may only be dickering about the amount. You're a specialist; maybe you don't need a lot of love from me. Maybe you only need a tiny bit. I think I could provide that.

KESS. Why did you try to kill Jo?

EVELYN. I didn't. I hit her.

KESS. She thinks you tried to...

EVELYN. You show me one mother who hasn't hit a child.

KESS. *(A beat.)* Well. I'm going to be here for a little while. I think Jo and Sherry could use whatever comfort and protection that would afford.

EVELYN. They do not need protection...

KESS. I think they do. I think they need that, and love.

EVELYN. You are just like Henry Briggs, you know that? Only here when you want to create new tragedies.

KESS. Mom...

EVELYN. You have all his false appeal and his seeming logic. But just like Henry, you become part of this family only when it suits you, and...

KESS. Mother...

EVELYN. And one day you will leave for good. Won't you? Won't you?

KESS. Why did you hit Jo?

EVELYN. I never hit Jo! *(Rising.)* I remember when a mother and daughter could converse like human beings about these things. You ask anybody in Independence about me. They'll say Evelyn Briggs is the sanest, most well-loved one among us. I am wonderful with those patients. I don't know what Jo may have told you, but it's...

KESS. *(Overlapping from "may.")* Jo has only been...

EVELYN. But it's not true! I am perfectly capable of functioning in a warm and loving universe. Which is what I try constantly to create!

JO. *(From off, in the kitchen.)* Mom! I'm back. I got your favorite! Cinnamon rolls!

EVELYN. I'd better go help Jo. Hope you like Constant Comment. *(She exits into the kitchen. Kess looks around the room, sighs and slumps on the arm of the couch. Lights fade to black.)*

Scene Two

Saturday morning, two days later. Lights rise to reveal Jo and Sherry. Jo is dressed, Sherry is still in her robe. Jo is singing from a book. She no longer wears the collar.

JO.
"It fell about the Martinmas
When nights are lang and mirk..."

SHERRY. *(Yawning.)* Swing it, sister.

JO. Sherry.

18

KESS. *(From the kitchen.)* Don't mind her. Keep going. You're good.

JO. I am not.

KESS. *(Off.)* Yes, you are.

JO. What's "lang and mirk" mean? "When nights are lang and mirk."

KESS. Long and murky — just like it sounds. *(Entering, with two cups of tea, one of which she gives to Jo. Like Jo, she is dressed.)* Martin- mas comes in the winter — so, naturally, long, dark nights. Go on. Your accent's great.

SHERRY. Yeah, great.

JO.
"The carline wife's three sons came hame..."

SHERRY. Came *hame?*

KESS. Sherry. It means home. "Carline" means old, by the way.

JO. Old? Carline means old?

KESS. Yup. It's there so we know she can't have any more children. See? Everything in a ballad has a purpose. That's why they're beautiful.

SHERRY. "That's why they're beautiful." Same old Kess. *(Sherry yawns.)*

KESS. Will you quit yawning?

SHERRY. I didn't get much sleep last night. Besides, I always yawn on Saturdays.

KESS. Go on, Jo.

JO. *(Sings.)*
"The carline wife's three sons came hame
And their hats were o' the birk."

SHERRY. What the hell does that mean?

KESS. It means they're dead.

JO. What?

KESS. Her three sons are dead. They're wearing hats made of birch. "Birk" means birch.

SHERRY. Oh, that explains it.

KESS. But there isn't any birch where she lives. And the next

19

verse indicates that while it doesn't grow there, it does grow at the gates of heaven.

JO. *(Beginning to get it.)* So...

KESS. So they're wearing hats made in heaven. See? They're dead. They were lost in a shipwreck three verses ago. Remember?

JO. How do you keep all this straight?

SHERRY. She doesn't. She makes it up.

KESS. The point is, we're dealing with ghosts here. This poor old woman has three sons, and she sends them all out sailing — major mistake — and word comes back they've drowned. Well, she doesn't want to believe *that*...

SHERRY. Why not?

KESS. So, some time later, they show up — surprisingly — and she's wild with joy. My sons are home! She doesn't notice the birch hats.

SHERRY. *I* would notice the birch hats.

KESS. She doesn't. She loves them, and she can't bear to think they're dead. So she welcomes them, and then she sits and watches over them all night long. But just before dawn she falls asleep. And they wake up before she does, and they leave her forever.

JO. That's awful. I mean it's pretty, but it's awful.

KESS. They can't help it. They have to get back to their graves.

SHERRY. Think I'll have an omelet.

JO. You always have an omelet.

SHERRY. It's all I can cook.

JO. Do you have any more songs?

KESS. Well, here's one about two crows eating a corpse...

JO. Oh ... not yet. Let me work up to that.

SHERRY. Seriously — who wants an omelet?

KESS. What kind?

SHERRY. Plain or lunchmeat.

KESS. No thanks. *(As Sherry exits into the kitchen.)* I'll make breakfast later. Are you taking those vitamins I gave you?

JO. Yeah.

KESS. How's the neck?

JO. *(Turning her head.)* 100%

KESS. Did you throw up today?

JO. Yup.

KESS. Good. We've got all sorts of progress in just two days. Now all we have to do is get you out exercising, instead of sitting around here all day reading drugstore novels.

JO. *Noble Incest* is not a drugstore novel. It's not a great novel...

KESS. We'll see if we can't find you something better.

JO. Kess? Is it fun? To be back?

KESS. Back with you? Yeah, sure it's fun.

JO. How about the town? The people?

KESS. This town? These people?

JO. Yeah.

KESS. Small-town living isn't for me.

JO. I think small towns are an important alternative to the stress of contemporary urban life.

KESS. *(Laughs.)* You do, do you?

JO. How long can you stay?

KESS. I told you. Till Monday.

JO. It's been such a relief to have you here. I really feel calm now. Mom's happier.

KESS. Not sure I believe *that*.

JO. She is. Really. Yesterday she said it's a lovely thing when a family reunites.

KESS. She didn't say it to me.

JO. But she said it. To somebody. That's progress.

KESS. You think that's progress, eh?

JO. Of course it is. It's not easy for her, you know. She has to go by little steps.

KESS. You know what I'd call progress? Real progress? If you were to decide — now that you're going to have a baby — to move up to Minneapolis with me.

JO. What?

KESS. Come and live with me.

21

JO. I couldn't do that.

KESS. Why not? Try and think about it rationally...

JO. I don't have to think about it rationally. I couldn't do that.

KESS. Why not?

JO. 'Cause I can't leave Mom. How can you even suggest it?

KESS. I'm only...

JO. What would happen to her? Tell me — what would happen?

KESS. She'd be all right.

JO. She would, huh? How?!

KESS. She's managed for 53 years.

JO. No, she hasn't. She's never managed alone. She's always needed someone. First there was her family, then Dad, then you after Dad left, then me. Who'd be here when I left? Not Sherry. Mom would be all alone.

KESS. *(A beat.)* So what?

JO. *So what?!*

KESS. I have a very big place in Minneapolis. There'd be room for you. My roommate wouldn't mind...

JO. You already asked your *roommate?* Jesus, Kess...

KESS. I had to know before I could...

JO. Is that the only reason you came down? To try and steal me away from Mom?

KESS. No, it's just that...

JO. If you think I'd leave Mom to move up there with you and that ... that...

KESS. That what?

JO. You know.

KESS. That what? That Susan, you mean. That's her name.

JO. I think we should just drop it.

KESS. *(With control, not defensive.) That* roommate — Susan — is the same as me. Our life is more normal than anything that goes on in this house.

SHERRY. *(Off.)* That's the truth.

KESS. Sher, if you want to join the conversation you can come in here.

22

SHERRY. *(Off.)* No, thanks.

JO. *(A beat.)* I'm sorry.

KESS. That's all right.

JO. I just know I can't go up there and leave Mom, that's all.

KESS. 'Cause she needs you.

JO. That's right.

KESS. What for? What does she need you for?

JO. Everything. She needs me to listen to her. She needs me to talk to her, to be with her — to be thinking about her. What does anybody need anybody for?

KESS. Shouldn't people sometimes ... change who they need?

JO. Mom's done that.

KESS. I don't mean Mom. I mean you.

JO. *(A beat.)* We're getting off the point.

KESS. What do you need from Mom?

JO. Nothing. I help her. She doesn't help me. Ok?

KESS. Something. You get something out of it.

JO. I don't get a thing. I give. That's my life. I give to people. There's nothing wrong with it. You should try it sometime.

KESS. I wasn't saying...

JO. It's easy for you. You just take what you need from people. You don't care how much you change in the process. You don't care if your whole family doesn't recognize you anymore when you... *(She stops herself, very embarrassed.)* I'm sorry.

KESS. That's all right.

JO. It's not true — we recognize you. You're always ... Kess. *(A beat. Kess sighs.)*

KESS. Well...

JO. Why don't you move down here?

KESS. What?

JO. Move back down. Be close to us.

KESS. I couldn't do that.

JO. Why not? You make changes. You could find a way. Bring Susan.

KESS. *Susan*...? Mom'd *love* that.

JO. You could work, you could find a job...

KESS. Jo ...

JO. You can do anything if you care enough.

KESS. Is that why you asked me down here? To steal me away from my life?

JO. I'm not stealing you away! I'm ... inviting you. You could do a lot of good down here. You could really provide something for Mom...

KESS. I do provide. I provide a hell of a lot, as you'll recall. Who was here to put Mom in the MHI when she needed it?

JO. Who was here when she got out? You were already gone. I was the one who took her around to say hello to everybody again. I took her into each store. I shopped with her.

KESS. I'm leaving on Monday.

JO. Go ahead — leave!

KESS. I will.

JO. Fine! *(A silence. Sherry enters, eating a Hostess Cupcake.)*

SHERRY. How are things in here? Everybody happy?

KESS. I thought you were having an omelet. What's that?

SHERRY. Dessert. This is getting to be a lively day. What with you guys yelling, and Mom.

KESS. What about Mom?

SHERRY. You didn't hear her dawn raid this morning? It was a beaut. She caught me with a boy.

JO. She's caught you with boys before.

SHERRY. Not with two boys.

JO. *Two* boys...?

SHERRY. Oh, it was just inane. I was only in bed with one of them.

JO. Well, who...?

SHERRY. Ed and Red Randall. *(To Kess.)* Ed's my boyfriend.

JO. What was Red doing there?

SHERRY. He came over to ask Ed a question, that's all. I think he wanted to borrow money, I don't know. It was still dark out. Anyway — it was so stupid — Red was crawling through the window, and he slipped on my dresser and made this incredible crash, and Mom came in. And there we were: all three of us on the bed. Well,

Red was kind of half on the floor.

JO. Oh, Sherry...

SHERRY. Mom must've been wandering around out here. She came right in, she was all dressed and everything. Anyway, she practically killed Ed and Red, thereby ruining my social life.

JO. What'd she do?

SHERRY. *(Laughs.)* She threw your picture at them. You know — your graduation picture. In the frame? *(Sherry points to a table where Kess and Sherry's framed pictures sit, with a noticeable gap between them.)*

JO. Oh, no.

SHERRY. Who knows why she was carrying it around with her?

JO. Where is it now?

SHERRY. All over my room. They were both scared shitless. They were out the window in two seconds. Then she screamed, "You'll thank me someday," and ran out.

JO. Where'd she go?

SHERRY. Who knows? Maybe she went and drowned herself.

JO. I'll check her room. *(Jo hurries upstairs.)*

KESS. Why didn't you tell us about this?

SHERRY. What's to tell? It's the way she always is.

KESS. Don't you care about her at all?

SHERRY. Don't you? I don't see you running upstairs. *(A moment passes. Jo returns.)*

JO. She's ... asleep. She's fine.

SHERRY. She's fine and Ed's terrified. *(Curling up on the couch.)* Be sure and tell me when you both finally sneak out on her for good. I don't want to be the last one out the door. *(She closes her eyes, napping. The others stare at her, then at each other. Lights fade to black.)*

Scene Three

Around noon, the same day. Jo is staring out a side window, toward the back of the house. We hear sweeping sounds from Sherry's room. After a moment, Evelyn emerges — a dustpan full of glass in one hand, a broom and a damaged photo in the other.

EVELYN. That takes care of that. At least your photo wasn't too badly torn. A little scotch tape... *(Evelyn moves toward the kitchen with the dustpan.)*

JO. I'm sorry you had to clean it up yourself.

EVELYN. No— Sherry has every right to demand that. I was the one who lost her temper. I made the mess. *(Evelyn disappears into the kitchen.)*

JO. She wouldn't let me clean it up. I offered to, but she just...

EVELYN. *(Off.)* It's fine, it's fine. Your heart was in the right place. *(Reentering, sans broom and dustpan, but with the picture.)* Have to get a new frame for this. *(Sets it on the table with the other photos.)* Such a sweet picture. I'm sorry it was yours I threw. But I was looking at it right when I heard those noises, and I just...

JO. That's ok, Mom.

EVELYN. Well, there's a basic level of trust. In any home.

JO. I know. Did you sleep well, this morning?

EVELYN. Like a dream. Lost half the day, but I don't care. Is Sherry around? Where is everyone?

JO. Kess went out for a run. Sherry's in the backyard.

EVELYN. *(Moving to the window Jo had been looking out.)* She is? What's she doing?

JO. Working on her sculpture.

EVELYN. Oh. Well. She should stop it.

JO. Tell her that.

EVELYN. It's so awful. And it's right next to Mrs. Anderberg's vegetable garden. She called and complained yesterday. Said if she'd only known what Sherry was going to do with those lawn ornaments, she'd never have sold them to her.

JO. Too late.

EVELYN. I said if she wanted to go ahead and sue Sherry, I'd back her up.

JO. Against your own daughter?

EVELYN. I'm not really sure Sherry is my daughter. I was so drugged up when I had her, they could've given me any baby and I wouldn't have known. *(Jo laughs. Evelyn smiles.)* It's nice, having you all in the house again. We're never all together in the same room, it seems, but at least we're all ... around. Do you like having her here?

JO. Who — Kess? Sure. It's wonderful.

EVELYN. *(A beat.)* It is, isn't it.

JO. Yes, it is.

EVELYN. I hope she's having a good time. I suppose she probably came down here expecting to find us locked in some sort of death struggle.

JO. She did not.

EVELYN. Lord knows what you told her.

JO. I didn't tell her anything.

EVELYN. You told her I hit you.

JO. You did hit me.

EVELYN. I did not. I struck out, that's all. I simply struck out against Fate, and there you were. It's not the same as hitting.

JO. It *felt* the...

EVELYN. It's not the same. *(A beat.)* There's not the same responsibility, is there?

JO. *(A beat.)* No.

EVELYN. *(Picking up a magazine.)* Kess has been talking to people in town about me. Did you know that? Mrs. Herold was angry about it. She really was. Kess walked up to her — hadn't seen her in years — and said, "How does my mother seem to you these days?". I can just hear her.

JO. I'm sure she didn't mean anything...

EVELYN. If I hadn't had the three of you so far apart we'd be more of a family. There'd be more of us in the room right now. Kess was nearly grown by the time Sherry was born. They must stare at each other like the Earth and the moon.

JO. Do you want some lunch...? *(Evelyn puts the magazine down.)*

EVELYN. Where were you Wednesday night?

JO. What?

EVELYN. Wednesday night. The night before Kess got here. Where did you go?

JO. Nowhere important.

EVELYN. Where, though?

JO. Nowhere.

EVELYN. You must've gone somewhere.

JO. I didn't go anywhere, all right? I really didn't.

EVELYN. I'm only curious.

JO. What's it matter?

EVELYN. I guess it doesn't.

JO. That's right. It doesn't matter. It doesn't matter at all.

EVELYN. *(A beat.)* Then why can't you tell me?

JO. *(Moving toward the stairs.)* I'm going to go change. Kess and I are going out when she gets back...

EVELYN. Mrs. Rowley says she saw you over at Don's house Wednesday night. *(Jo stops.)* Is that where you were? Don's house?

JO. Yes.

EVELYN. You went over there, and you never told me?

JO. There was nothing to tell. He wasn't home.

EVELYN. Oh. You were gone a long time.

JO. I know. I just ... sort of sat on his step for awhile.

EVELYN. *(A beat.)* Why?

JO. I ... thought he might come home.

EVELYN. No — I mean, why did you go see him?

JO. No reason.

EVELYN. There's always some reason. There must have been

some reason.

JO. I wanted to see if he felt like going out, all right?

EVELYN. You didn't call him first?

JO. It was kind of a whim.

EVELYN. I thought you and Don were finished.

JO. We are; so what? *(A beat.)* He's dating other people. I sat for half an hour on his step. Folks walked by and said, "Hi, Jo. Don's out tonight, you know." I said, "I know." They all looked at me like I was ... what I was. So I came home.

EVELYN. *(Moving to her, sitting close.)* I've missed you these last weeks. I'm glad we're not fighting anymore. Aren't you? *(Jo nods. Evelyn takes her hand.)* Sometimes a man comes into your life, and you think it's the answer to your problems, but you always find out it's not. Henry was just a man. He didn't care about me. He was handsome, and he was fine while there was enough money, or there was enough whatever, but in the end he didn't care.

JO. I know.

EVELYN. I'll be glad when Sherry's gone. I shouldn't say that, but I will. Then it'll just be you and me. Won't that be fun? *(Jo nods.)* We'll have Kess and Sherry visit now and then, of course. But mostly, it'll just be us. I rely on you. So few people in the world can really be relied on. Don't you think? So few things. I've lived in this house my entire life. Do you realize that?

JO. It amazes me sometimes.

EVELYN. You too. You've lived in it all yours.

JO. Yes.

EVELYN. Kess will be gone on Monday. Then Sherry will go. Just you and me. At last. *(A beat.)* I'm wearing my cameo.

JO. What?

EVELYN. I'm wearing my cameo. Did you notice?

JO. Oh ... it's lovely. I'm sorry, I didn't notice.

EVELYN. That's because you haven't been looking at me. In the craft center they tell us to look squarely at the patients — at least at those who'll look squarely at us — and to smile, and to be encouraging. I think that's good advice for life in general, don't you? *(Of the cameo.)* It's a beautiful thing, isn't it? Family heirlooms always are.

JO. Yes.

EVELYN. Henry, your father, and I used to drive to Des Moines once a month when you were little. He went on business — allegedly— and I went to shop. After we'd done this for over a year, he suddenly looked at me on the way home one day and said, "What's that?". I said, "It's my cameo." "Where did you get it?" he asked. "I've had it for seven years," I told him. "Why haven't you ever worn it before?". "I wear it all the time," I said, "It's my dearest possession." He was just silent then, the whole way home. Never said he was sorry. *(Unpinning the cameo, examining it.)* That was the first time I ever felt sorry for him, though. Must be strange for a man, to live in a world full of only big things.

JO. You used to show it to Kess and me.

EVELYN. I did, didn't I?

JO. You let us hold it.

EVELYN. *(Starts to hand it to Jo, then suddenly pulls it back for reexamination.)* You two fought over it. Didn't you?

JO. Some fight. Kess always won. *(Evelyn pins the cameo back on herself.)* You haven't had it on in ages. Why are you wearing it now?

EVELYN. So I don't forget to give it to Kess.

JO. You're giving it to Kess?

EVELYN. Well, I know I talked about giving it to you. But that was when I was mad at Kess, and thought she wasn't a part of us anymore.

JO. Kess is getting the...?

EVELYN. You know, I thought of it just as I woke up. It's truly the perfect idea. After all, Kess has been so much calmer this trip. We need to give her something. And what better than the cameo? It's hers by rights. She is the oldest.

JO. But..

EVELYN. I know — I'm breaking tradition, to give it to her before I die. But I thought it might be just the message she needs to see that ... I love her, and I'm all right. Do you think she'll like it?

JO. *(A beat.)* Of course. It's lovely.

EVELYN. It is, isn't it? I remember when your Aunt Elaine died, and I got it. Do you realize this cameo has been owned by women in our family for over 150 years? Imagine. I'm sorry I don't have one for you, too. But Kess has to live far away. We can give her this to remind her of us. You're right here. You have me. *(A beat.)* I'll tell you something else. Now that Don is... well, moving in another direction, I think you and I have a special opportunity — one that a mother and daughter rarely get. We have the chance to give each other something far more valuable than a cameo.

JO. What?

EVELYN. Our lives. *(A long beat. Evelyn kisses Jo on the forehead. Jo is motionless.)* Now, where can I leave this?

JO. Leave it?

EVELYN. I know! On her table upstairs. She'll find it when she goes up tonight. *(She goes for the stairs.)*

JO. Well ... if you're going to give it to her, why don't you give it to her?

EVELYN. No, no, no. This is better. A surprise.

JO. It's ridiculous, giving her the cameo like that.

EVELYN. You don't understand — it'll be lovely. Look: I sneak in her room, leave it on her table. She walks in, wanders around, comes over to the table and... You see? It'll be very special.

JO. That's not special.

EVELYN. Of course it is.

JO. Putting it in her hand and looking her in the eye — that would be special. Leaving it on a table is lousy.

EVELYN. No, it's lovely. You just don't see it.

JO. I would never want to get a gift that way. Especially that gift. From my own mother...

EVELYN. Kess will adore getting this gift in just this way. And no amount of jealous carping...

JO. I'm not jealous! I'm not!

EVELYN. No one knows Kess the way I do. And I am going up this minute and leaving this cameo right on her goddamn table, is that clear?!

JO. Yes.

EVELYN. Good. Kess is my oldest. She and I communicate in ways you and Sherry would not understand.

JO. Yes, Mom. *(Evelyn starts to exit, stops.)*

EVELYN. It will be a lovely gesture. From the both of us. *(Evelyn exits upstairs. Jo stares after her a moment, as lights fade to black.)*

Scene Four

Sunday evening, the next day. Sherry at a table, with a pile of slides in front of her. She looks at them one by one as she speaks, dividing them into two piles. Kess, wearing the cameo, sits on the couch, looking through a book.

SHERRY. So what I'm saying is, he was fantastic, that's all.

JO. *(Off, in Sherry's room.)* He was, was he?

SHERRY. Of course he was. He's from New York. He's a biker. I met him at the bar last night.

KESS. *(Absently.)* Sounds very attractive.

SHERRY. Yeah, he's an artist.

KESS. *(Calling out.)* How about Standish?

JO. *(Off.)* What?

KESS. Standish. That might be all right.

JO. *(Off.)* Are you kidding? *Standish?*

SHERRY. I can't believe you guys are actually picking baby names.

KESS. We actually are. *(Calling.)* How about Hannibal?

JO. *(Off.)* No. Sherry, where's your black top?

SHERRY. On the closet door.

JO. *(Off.)* Oh — thanks!

SHERRY. *(To Kess.)* Don't you want to hear about this guy I met?

KESS. No. *(Sherry suddenly steals Kess's book.)*

SHERRY. Well, do — 'cause he's real interesting.

KESS. Sherry...!

SHERRY. Come on. You can do baby names later. This guy is a grown-up.

KESS. I don't have time. I'm going home tomorrow.

SHERRY. So what? Mail it in. *(Kess grabs for the book. Sherry pulls it away and sits on it. A standoff.)*

KESS. Jo, she's got the book.

JO. *(Off.)* Sherry...

SHERRY. Jo — try my black shoes, too. They're on the stereo. One of 'em is, anyway.

JO. *(Off.)* Oh — yeah. Thanks!

SHERRY. No problem. *(To Kess.)* So. First of all, he's very aloof. Like he's not from here, right?

KESS. *(Looking irritably at Sherry's room.)* Where's he from?

SHERRY. New York. Don't you listen? Like I said he's a biker.

KESS. Charming.

SHERRY. He's got this great big Harley that looks like it eats rabbits. And he's got leathers and chains... And he's got tattoos.

JO. *(Off.)* Tattoos?

SHERRY. On both arms! Plus a little one on his nose. It's like this little vine or something, curling around one nostril. Want to know what his job is?

KESS. *(Leaning in the doorway to Sherry's room, staring into it.)* No.

JO. *(Off.)* Yes!

SHERRY. He's an insect photographer.

JO. *(Off.)* A what?

SHERRY. He takes close-up shots of insects — like in Walt Disney movies and stuff. He's got this butterfly net on his bike. I saw it.

KESS. Jo, do you really think you should wear that?

JO. *(Entering, wearing a showy black top.)* Why not?

KESS. You don't know what Don's coming over for, exactly.

JO. He's taking me out. He said. "Can we go someplace?" Those were his exact words. Sherry, do you like it?

SHERRY. Yeah, on me. *(A beat. They stare at Jo.)*

JO. Well ... I thought maybe he'll want to go to a restaurant or something. *(A beat. Jo's confidence crumbles. She goes back into Sherry's room.)*

SHERRY. Anyway, this guy's one of Disney's biggest suppliers. That's what he told me, at least. You know what insect he hates to film?

KESS. I give completely up.

SHERRY. The praying mantis.

JO. *(Off.)* What about the green?

KESS. Jo...

SHERRY. He says everybody does that. Every nature movie has a praying mantis in it. You ever notice that?

KESS. Sherry...

SHERRY. And it's always the same shot: praying mantis sits there not moving; praying mantis grabs something faster than you can see it anyway; praying mantis eats it; praying mantis sits there not moving again. It's a limited insect.

JO. *(Off.)* I'm wearing this one.

KESS. I don't think...

JO. *(Off.)* Forget it. My mind's made up.

SHERRY. You know what he likes better? The dung beetle. They're more inventive. They roll these little balls of dung all over hell, you know?

KESS. I know.

SHERRY. They're very creative. Anyway, like I say, this guy's an artist, and I showed him some slides of sculptures I made, and he liked 'em, *and* he's taking 'em to New York with him. To try and make me famous — you know? I'm sending him more tomorrow. Want to see 'em?

KESS. No.

JO. *(Off.)* What's his name?

SHERRY. What?

KESS. Has the Hell's Angel insect photographer art connoisseur got a name?

SHERRY. Spinner. Isn't that great? We only knew each other a couple hours. It was kind of a lightning relationship. *(Hands Kess her book back.)* Just thought you'd be interested. *(Jo reenters in a top that's slightly more demure, but still is too dressy.)*

JO. This is it. How do I look?

SHERRY. Like Heidi Joy Duckly.

JO. Well, I don't care. It's what I'm wearing.

KESS. Jo, you don't even know where you're going.

JO. We're going somewhere. That's all that matters.

KESS. Why not stay here? You two could talk here.

JO. *(Going to the front window, looking out.)* Oh, brilliant idea.

KESS. When's he coming?

JO. A half hour. *(Moving to the couch.)* I can't believe he called. Someone must've told him I was at his house.

SHERRY. Yeah, like half of town.

JO. I don't care.

KESS. Jo, is Don really worth getting this excited about?

JO. I'm not excited.

KESS. It's just that ... for all the trouble he's caused...

JO. What trouble?

KESS. Mom tonight, for one thing.

JO. Well ... I can't help Mom. We already had one fight over it, and that's it. She's all right now.

KESS. She's out cleaning up the garage. At seven in the evening. Does that sound like she's all right?

JO. It's not my fault if she loses her temper! You should be happy I'm getting away from her.

KESS. I am, but...

JO. You're just mad 'cause it's your last night here, and I'm going out. I understand that. And I'm sorry, but...

KESS. I just wish you'd be a little less frantic about it.

JO. How do you expect me to be? Don called up. Maybe he wants to ask me to get married.

SHERRY. What if he does? You'll just say no again.

JO. I will not.

SHERRY. Will he agree to live with Mom? Will he even come in the house?

35

JO. I'll leave Mom.

SHERRY. Sure.

JO. I wish he'd get here.

KESS. Relax.

JO. Maybe he'll take me to a movie. We like doing that. Sher, what's on in town?

SHERRY. The new James Bond.

JO. James Bond! God. Great. Remember when we used to go to those as kids?

KESS. Yeah. Mom used to take us.

SHERRY. Sure. They were the only movies a 20-year-old, a 12-year-old and a 6-year-old all liked.

JO. That's right. Remember, we'd all sit there eating out of those red and white striped popcorn boxes, and Mom would lean over us and say, "Watch James Bond. Watch the way he acts around women. Watch what happens to the women..."

KESS, JO and SHERRY. *(Together.)* "They al-l-l-l-l-l-l die." *(They laugh.)*

SHERRY. God, we all remember.

JO. "They al-l-l-l-l-l-l die." Just like that. What happened to the woman in that movie, anyway? Didn't she fall into a car-masher or something?

KESS. I think so.

JO. Yeah. *(A beat. They grow silent.)*

KESS. *(Sighs.)* Ok, ok, ok. Go out with him. Have a good time. Get frantic if you want to.

JO. Thanks. So — um... *(Indicates the book.)* Pick more baby names.

SHERRY. Do we have to?

KESS. All right. What about, um ... Lanier.

JO. Lanier? I don't know.

SHERRY. Could we please do anything else?

KESS. What about Banquo?

JO. Will you quit it?

SHERRY. How about Shulamith?

JO. Give me a girl's name. It's going to be a girl.

SHERRY. Shulamith is a girl's name.

KESS. Let's see: Marina.

JO. No.

KESS. Chloe.

JO. Are you ignoring all the common ones?

KESS. Who needs a book for Mary? Annabella.

SHERRY. Have we really, honestly considered Shulamith?

JO. Sherry...

SHERRY. Hey — how about Merlin?

JO. *Mer*lin? Why?

SHERRY. 'Cause then he could make himself disappear.

JO. He's not going to disappear! He's going to be born, and have a mother and a father!

SHERRY. Yeah, who?

JO. *Me and Don!*

SHERRY. Oh, wake up! He's probably coming over to tell you to keep off his porch!

KESS. Sherry!

SHERRY. And you — you're a bigger idiot than Jo! Picking *baby* names. I noticed you never picked one for mine.

KESS. What good would that have done?

SHERRY. It might've helped me keep it.

KESS. You were 15 years old.

SHERRY. I was old enough! You had to pry it away from me with a stick!

KESS. *I'm glad I had a stick! (A beat. Kess puts down the book.)* Let's not do this.

SHERRY. *(Quietly.)* I gave her a name myself, anyway. Shulamith. 'Course she's probably called Barbie or Cathy by now.

KESS. Wherever she is, she's in a better family than this.

SHERRY. How would you know? You only come down when you feel like it. *(Flicking Kess's cameo.)* You just drop in now and then, pick up whatever you want, and leave.

KESS. Oh — I suppose you wanted it too, huh?

SHERRY. No, but Jo did.

JO. I did not.

KESS. *(To Sherry.)* I come down here because you three can't get along without me. Eventually you always have a disaster.

SHERRY. Maybe we like disasters!

JO. You *guys*...

SHERRY. I can't believe it. You don't care any more about this family than I do — but everybody looks up to you. Everybody's afraid of you. And meanwhile I'm supposed to be this little *shit*...

KESS. Well put! *(Sherry gives an angry yell and pushes Kess onto the couch. They struggle.)*

JO. Kess! Sherry! Stop it!! Let go! LET GO!! *(As they fight, Evelyn enters via the kitchen. She is disheveled, bleeding, frightened.)*

EVELYN. Kess? Kess?

JO. *(Looking around.)* Oh, God — *Mom! (The others look up.)*

EVELYN. Kess, I'm hurt.

JO. *(Rushing to her, as the others rise.)* What happened?

EVELYN. *(Moving into Kess's arms.)* I was cleaning the garage. I ... found the old dishes. The old china. I think I ... broke something. I couldn't hold onto the plates... *(Kess and Jo move her to a chair. Sherry runs out through the kitchen.)*

JO. I'll get a towel. *(Jo exits into the kitchen.)*

EVELYN. There was just me. There was ... I was all alone out there.

KESS. Calm down, now. Everything's all right. You're with me. *(Jo reenters with a towel.)*

EVELYN. I kept seeing Jo. She wasn't ... there, but she ... I saw her.

JO. Are those her only cuts?

KESS. I think so.

JO. Here, let me wrap this around. *(Sherry reenters.)*

SHERRY. Geez— I don't believe it. The garage is full of broken dishes. Everywhere you look

EVELYN. I was completely alone. *(A car horn honks outside.)*

JO. Oh, God — Don! *(Moving toward the front door.)* Um ... um... *(The horn honks again.)* Kess, I ... that's Don ... I... *(She suddenly bolts out the front door.)*

EVELYN. Where's she going?

KESS. It's all right.

EVELYN. But where's...?

KESS. Why did you break the dishes?

EVELYN. What?

KESS. Why did you break the dishes?

EVELYN. They were in my hand.

SHERRY. How bad are her cuts?

KESS. Not bad. Mom, were you throwing them at someone?

EVELYN. Yes.

KESS. Who? Who were you throwing them at? *(Jo reenters from the front.)*

JO. Mom? I sent him away. I told him I couldn't see him, all right? Mom? I sent Don away. He's gone. He's all gone.

EVELYN. *(Quietly.)* I threw them at Jo. *(Lights fade to black.)*

END OF ACT ONE

ACT TWO
Scene One

Lights rise on Kess and Evelyn, in robes, sitting at a table. They are playing Scrabble. *Late Thursday evening, four days later.*

EVELYN. I used to sit around this table with my own sisters. You know that? I remember many times we'd sit around this same room, and just talk for hours. Mostly about our friends. Well, their friends, really. I was much younger. We'd stay up whole nights. This house. My mother was born in it.

KESS. Do you allow Greek letter words?

EVELYN. Like what?

KESS. Alpha, beta, pi.

EVELYN. No. *(A beat.)* Staying up nights. I always loved that when I was young. Now I wish I could sleep.

KESS. You slept last night, didn't you?

EVELYN. Oh, yes. I'm much calmer than I was. You've been so good to me all week. I'm sorry I made you change your plans, but I'm glad you're staying longer.

KESS. I just want to make sure you're feeling better. I mean, since your...

EVELYN. My smash up? Oh, yes. I feel much better. Actually, that let off a lot of steam for me. I scared myself, I admit, but now I'm almost glad it happened. And I won't miss those dishes. They were terrible old things. You almost make me feel like a princess, you've paid so much attention to me since. I hope it hasn't been hard on you.

KESS. Agony.

EVELYN. Really? That bad?

KESS. *(Putting letters on the board.)* No, that's the word I'm playing. "Agony." Let's see: that's one-two-three-four-five-six-seven-eight-nine. Plus a double word score. Eighteen.

EVELYN. Who's ahead?

KESS. I am.

EVELYN. Really? By how much?

KESS. Um ... 380 points.

EVELYN. Oh... *(Playing.)* "Me." *(Kess looks at her.)* That's what I'm playing.

KESS. *(Recording the score.)* Four points.

EVELYN. I think it's so sweet of you to babysit me while your sisters have a night out.

KESS. They've had three nights out.

EVELYN. Well, they need it. What with Jo having that new disappointment with Don. I think she's lost all her chances there, don't you? You can't keep telling someone to go away, and expect them to keep coming back. Has she tried to call him again?

KESS. *(Nods.)* Mm-hmm. He's never home, though.

EVELYN. Well. We're certainly home, aren't we? Just a couple old maids, home for the night. *(As Kess works out a move.)* How am I?

KESS. What?

EVELYN. Do you think I'm in trouble?

KESS. What do you mean?

EVELYN. In the game.

KESS. Oh — can you win? No, you can't.

EVELYN. Ah. *(A beat.)* Do you like the cameo? I've noticed you wear it a lot.

KESS. It's beautiful. Thanks again.

EVELYN. You're welcome. Is it fun having a family again? It must be wonderful to rediscover your sisters this way. I remember my own sisters. I used to have such sweet memories of them, mostly. *(Indicating the room.)* We used to sleep right in here, sometimes. All of us, together. On hot summer nights. You going to play soon?

KESS. Pretty soon.

EVELYN. We would take sheets — all of us — and we'd open all

41

the windows and the porch door and turn on the fan, and sleep on our wonderful white heaven of bare sheets.

KESS. How about solmizations?

EVELYN. What?

KESS. Do, re, mi, fa, sol...

EVELYN. No, I don't allow those. Anyway, it was such an adventure for me. There I was, the baby of the family, trying to stay awake while they were all trying to go to sleep.

KESS. Uh-huh.

EVELYN. All night I would stare right along the floor, under the davenport. I don't know what I ever expected to see there. And in the morning I'd wake up, and someone would have turned off the fan, and it would be cold some mornings, if a front had gone through. And there I'd be: wrapped in a sheet, with Elaine's — she was my favorite sister — with Elaine's arms around me. That's the loveliest waking-up memory I have, and I was married for almost 16 years.

KESS. Come back to the table.

EVELYN. Have you got a play?

KESS. Just about.

EVELYN. *(Sitting again.)* I think we go at different paces. I like to play a lot of games of *Scrabble* in one sitting. You make each game a work of art.

KESS. *(Playing two letters.)* Let's see ... if I do this, it's four this way for "gal," 35 for "maze," and 37 for "hazel" because of the two triple-letter scores ... which makes a grand total of ... 76.

EVELYN. "Up."

KESS. Four points. Mom, are you enjoying this? We don't have to play if you don't want.

EVELYN. What else would we do?

KESS. Well ... I guess we could play a little longer.

EVELYN. Why not? *(As Kess considers her next move.)* You know, the other night, when I was... throwing those dishes? I imagined Jo was there.

KESS. I know. You told me.

EVELYN. All around me, sort of. It was her I was throwing the dishes at I knew I was imagining — I wasn't confused about that. But it was very vividly her. All those dishes.

KESS. Do you really want to go into it?

EVELYN. No. *(A beat.)* You're my quietest child. You always have been. Sherry talks with every breath, but you never tell me anything, really, about yourself. Mrs. O'Connor saw you the other day.

KESS. Mrs. O'Connor?

EVELYN. You remember her. Your fourth-grade teacher? Always smiles and wears purple? Large teeth? Anyway, she said she still remembers you from then — just the way you were: stiff as a little post, quiet as could be.

KESS. I was not stiff.

EVELYN. Oh, yes you were. She remembers it. She said it was just like you were dead, only you could move from place to place. Isn't that an odd way to put it? I can see what she means, though. Do you have a move? What are you doing?

KESS. *(Having begun to cry silently.)* Nothing.

EVELYN. Are you crying?

KESS. No, I'm fine.

EVELYN. You are. You're crying and you're not making a sound. How do you do that? Cry silently like that. You always cry that way.

KESS. I do not cry silently! I cry out loud like everyone else.

EVELYN. Such a quiet one.

KESS. I was not quiet. You just couldn't hear me.

EVELYN. You were out of the house before I even knew you were that way. "Gay," I mean. Did you know? Back then?

KESS. Of course.

EVELYN. Really? How early?

KESS. Always. There wasn't much I could do about it around here.

EVELYN. Well, of course not. I should hope not.

KESS. There were some things. The woods, for example.

EVELYN. The woods?

KESS. When you were like me, the woods were the only place you could... *(Evelyn suddenly rises.)*

EVELYN. I have to use the bathroom, dear. You go on talking if you want. *(She exits for the bathroom.)*

KESS. *(As she goes.)* Hey, you asked me. I'm willing to tell you. I will tell you. Mom... *(But Evelyn is gone. Kess waits a beat, then goes on in a loud voice.)* I hated the woods. I hated the birds and trees and spiders and ... ticks. But when you're sixteen, and you want a lover — and it has to be a girl or you wouldn't be in love — you have to become a YWCA counselor and go to the woods. And just hope some other YWCA counselor is there for the same reason. And pray that people don't find out about you and fire you because they think you want to sleep with eight-year-old campers or something. I spent three summers lying terrified in a puptent for one affair that lasted two weeks, with a counselor I didn't even like. *(A beat.)* Mom? I know you can hear me.

EVELYN. *(Off.)* Go ahead and play. I'll be right out. *(Kess picks up the board and pours the letters into the box. Evelyn reenters.)*

KESS. Hi.

EVELYN. Did you win?

KESS. It was a tie.

EVELYN. I don't know what happened. Nature just suddenly called, loud and clear. *(A beat.)* So. What'll we do now?

KESS. Whatever you like.

EVELYN. *(Her eyes suddenly lighting up.)* Let's bake!

KESS. Bake?

EVELYN. Sure. We'll make something fun, for when the girls get home.

KESS. It's getting late...

EVELYN. Oh, come on. Remember when we used to do that? On nights your father was ... when he was out? Jo'd be sleeping upstairs, and you and I would bake for hours together. Biscuits, rolls, cookies — whatever we liked. It would get so late, but you never wanted to stop. I'd say something about the time, and you'd just go, "Ssshhh," and we'd keep on baking.

KESS. Mom...

EVELYN. Or I'd say, "Let's wake up Jo and give her some," and you'd shake your head *no*. Very firmly. Remember how it was? Just the two of us, late at night, like the real bakers?

KESS. *(A beat.)* All right, let's bake.

EVELYN. Good! *(Moves toward the kitchen.)* I can't tell you what having you back has meant, Kess. You give me back my sense of control. *(Suddenly we hear Sherry and Jo outside the porch.)*

SHERRY. *(Off, drunkenly.)* Come on, Jo — can't you recognize your own house?

JO. *(Off, drunkenly.)* It looks different.

SHERRY. *(Helping her through the front door.)* Believe me, this is it. Hi. We're drunk.

KESS. Jo, you said you weren't going to drink.

JO. *(Collapsing on the couch.)* I didn't.

SHERRY. Relax. She only had two beers.

JO. Two and a half.

SHERRY. You shouldn't have had any. Maybe then you wouldn't've been such a social disaster.

JO. I was not a social disaster.

EVELYN. Jo, are you all right?

JO. I'm fine. Am I lying down?

EVELYN. *(To Sherry.)* What is wrong with her?

SHERRY. Nothing. She flopped, that's all.

EVELYN. Flopped?

JO. Sherry fixed me up. Do you believe it? My little sister fixed me up. With the bartender.

KESS. Sherry, what did you...?

SHERRY. He's a terrific guy. Really easy to work with. At least he was.

JO. He was so handsome. Wasn't he?

SHERRY. You blew it. You froze up every time he talked to you.

JO. I couldn't talk to a man that beautiful.

SHERRY. You wasted two hours of his time. He was really trying. I never saw him work so hard. He liked you, stupid. *(To the others.)* She was just sitting there like Helen Keller all through it. Finally he says, "Look — I've asked you 50 questions. How about one answer?" Know what she says? "I'm pregnant." She told him she was pregnant.

JO. He asked what I did.

SHERRY. Bartenders are not looking for pregnant women. It's a well-known fact. They don't find them attractive.

JO. I thought I had a special glow.

SHERRY. Yeah, well you glowed him right out of your life. Why do you put all that on somebody when all you want is to get laid?

JO. I did not want to get laid.

SHERRY. There's nothing wrong with it. Some people even like it. *(Suddenly Evelyn throws the* Scrabble *game to the floor. The letters scatter. They look at her. She smiles sweetly, with genuine embarrassment.)*

EVELYN. I'm getting a little tired. Maybe I'd better go to bed.

KESS. Mom, no ... you don't have to...

EVELYN. That's all right.

JO. I wasn't really trying to get ... you know.

EVELYN. I know. That's all right. Good night.

KESS. We were going to bake...

EVELYN. Another time. *(To Sherry.)* I'm glad you got her home alive. *(Evelyn exits to the stairs.)*

KESS. Good going.

SHERRY. I didn't throw it.

KESS. *(To Jo.)* You too.

JO. I'm pregnant and I'm proud. *(Kess starts picking up the* Scrabble *game.)*

SHERRY. You're pregnant and you're dateless. God, look at us. It's 10:30 and we're home.

KESS. Sherry, help me with this.

SHERRY. Are you kidding? Get Mom to.

JO. *(Rolling off the couch, onto the floor.)* I'll help.

SHERRY. *(Watching them.)* I can't believe it. This is what I get? After three nights of intense therapy?

KESS. Therapy? You've been taking her out to bars.

SHERRY. I've been introducing her to alternative lifestyles. She's the one who wanted to go.

JO. I just want to forget about Don.

KESS. There are better ways.

SHERRY. No, there aren't. Meet new guys. It's the code I live by.

KESS. Yeah, right.

JO. He really was good-looking.

KESS. Wonderful.

SHERRY. What are you mad about? Jo enjoyed herself tonight. She didn't walk around all mopey like she does here.

KESS. How does it feel to be eternally thirteen?

SHERRY. Great. And I'll tell you what else feels great. Getting Jo out of this house and away from a crazy woman.

KESS. *Mom is not a crazy woman.*

SHERRY. She isn't? You don't think it's crazy, trying to kill yourself with a dinner set?

KESS. You heard Dr. Hanson the same as I did. The same as all of us did.

SHERRY. You think I believe a man who's only seen her once?

KESS. He works with her out there.

SHERRY. But he only looked at her once! Yesterday. And I'm supposed to believe him when he says, "Oh, her behavior's just a little extreme — she's not really deeply emotionally disturbed?"

KESS. Yes!

SHERRY. Well, I think it's bullshit. He just doesn't want to be near her, either.

KESS. *(A beat.)* He said, if you'll recall, that she doesn't need to be committed. She just needs to work out some problems here, with us. I think that could happen a lot faster if you guys would stop going out every night.

SHERRY. What do you think we should do? Sit around and have tea all day?

KESS. It might help.

SHERRY. Wonderful. We have tea for a week, and then you

leave for Minnesota again.

KESS. Who says I'm leaving in a week?

SHERRY. You have to go back sometime. Face it, Kess, you can't do her any good.

KESS. What good are you doing her?

SHERRY. *I'm* ignoring her. *(A beat.)* Who did you come down here for, anyway? I thought it was Jo.

KESS. *(Tiredly.)* Everybody. I came down for everybody.

SHERRY. I think you came down for you. *(A beat.)* To hell with this, I'm going to dance. *(Sherry moves toward her room.)*

JO. Oh ... Sherry, *no...*

SHERRY. *(Disappearing into her room.)* Why not? Time for music!

JO. You always play it too loud...

SHERRY. *(Off.)* Too loud? You're crazy! *(Loud rock music suddenly issues forth. Sherry reenters, as Kess exits into the kitchen.)*

JO. This is not considerate!

SHERRY. *(Dancing.)* Why? 'Cause it's what I like?

JO. You do this all the time! *(As they speak, Kess reenters, carrying a pair of scissors, such that Sherry doesn't see them. Kess goes into Sherry's room. The music stops.)*

SHERRY. Hey! Turn that back on! *(Kess returns, with the scissors.)* What are you doing?

KESS. *(Working the scissors.)* You need new speaker wires.

SHERRY. *What?!* *(She hurries into her room. Kess looks at Jo on her way upstairs.)*

KESS. I'll expect everybody for tea at 5 tomorrow.

JO. Kess... *(But Kess disappears upstairs.)*

SHERRY. *(Off.)* You're a *barbarian!* *(Reentering.)* Where is she?

JO. She went up...

SHERRY. *(Starting for the stairs.)* I'll kill her!

JO. *(Grabbing her.)* Sherry, stop...!

SHERRY. You screwed-up, over-achieving dyke!

JO. *(Holding her.)* Sherry...

SHERRY. *I'm gonna rip up all your books!*

48

JO. Sherry, let's do something fun, ok?

SHERRY. *I'm gonna blow up your car!*

JO. Sherry...!

SHERRY. *You hear me!?*

JO. Let's do something fun! Please? Let's just do something fun! *(Lights fade quickly to black.)*

Scene Two

Friday afternoon, the next day. Kess and Evelyn enter from the kitchen. Kess carries tea for four on a tray, which she sets on a low table near the couch.

KESS. *(In a loud voice, as she enters.)* Come on, everybody. This is going to be fun.

EVELYN. Where should I sit?

KESS. Anywhere. Wherever you're comfortable. *(Evelyn looks dubiously at all potential seats. Kess points out a chair.)* How about there?

EVELYN. *(Sitting.)* All right.

KESS. Sherry? Jo? You coming?

SHERRY. *(Off, in the kitchen.)* We're thinking about it.

KESS. Come on, come on — the tea'll get cold. *(To Evelyn.)* You want cream, right?

EVELYN. Thanks.

KESS. *(Sing-song.)* Sher-ry, Jo-o...

SHERRY. *(Entering in a dirty shirt and jeans, mimicking Kess's tone.)* All ri-ight, we're com-ing.

JO. *(Entering, neatly dressed.)* Where do you want us to sit?

KESS. Wherever you like. *(Sherry and Jo look around dubiously. Kess points out two places.)* Ok, you: there. You: there. *(They sit.)* Everyone comfortable? How do you want your tea?

SHERRY. In my room.

KESS. Jo?

JO. Just plain.

KESS. *(Handing a cup to Jo, then Sherry.)* Fine. Sherry? *(Sherry pauses, then takes a cup.)* Good. Now. Here we are — just as Dr. Hanson suggested — all four of us, sitting down together. First, I want to thank you all for agreeing to try.

SHERRY. I'm only doing it to show I can. Besides, I'm tired of working on my sculpture.

KESS. That's ok. Dr. Hanson said it's more important to go through the motions of being a happy family than it is to actually feel like one — at least, at this point. The more we act like a normal, happy family, the better the chance we'll become one someday. The new way of behaving will become as natural and unavoidable as the old, bad way.

SHERRY. I like the old bad way.

KESS. I know. But for now, let's act nice. Ok? As an experiment. So — who'd like to be the first to say something nice? *(A long silence.)*

EVELYN. The tea is very good.

KESS. Thank you. That's a good start. Would anyone else like to offer something positive? *(Another awkward silence.)*

JO. I like my cup. I mean, I've always liked these cups, ever since you got them.

EVELYN. Thank you.

KESS. Good. Anyone else? *(A beat.)* Sherry, I think I'm getting to like your sculpture.

SHERRY. Fuck you.

JO. *Sherry...*

SHERRY. I didn't raise my voice.

KESS. That's not the point.

SHERRY. Well, you're only saying that. You don't like my stuff any more than anyone else.

KESS. I know, but I'm pretending to.

SHERRY. Then you're just lying.

KESS. That's right.

SHERRY. Why?

KESS. *To be nice!! (With more control.)* Sorry. Please — just say thank you, ok? You don't have to know what it means; you don't have to feel it. Just say it. *(A beat. Sherry rises.)*

SHERRY. No way.

JO. Why not?

SHERRY. *(Moving towards her room.)* This is stupid. I don't want to do this.

KESS. You mean, you can't do it.

SHERRY. *(Stopping by her door.)* I can do it.

KESS. No, you can't.

SHERRY. I can.

KESS. Prove it.

SHERRY. *(A beat. With extreme unpleasantness.)* Thank you, Kess. That was a lovely compliment about my sculpture.

KESS. You're welcome. Wouldn't you like to come sit down again?

SHERRY. I'll stand.

KESS. That's fine with me — everybody else?

JO. Sure.

EVELYN. Sherry can do what she likes. She always does.

SHERRY. You call that positive?!

KESS. Mom, I thought we agreed to try this.

EVELYN. Aren't I doing it right?

KESS. Let's start over. How about if each of us talks about something she's doing, and then the rest of us find a positive comment to make about it? How would that be?

SHERRY. Stupid.

KESS. Sherry, why don't you tell about your sculpture? What do you like about it most?

SHERRY. It's grotesque.

KESS. *(Forging ahead.)* Ok. Grotesque. Good. Why do you like that?

SHERRY. It scares Mrs. Anderberg. Ever since I put the little fawn and the stable boy together in an unnatural act. Makes her weed her garden a lot faster.

KESS. Does anyone have anything ... positive to say about that?

JO. Well ... weeding faster is probably good exercise.

KESS. Good, Jo. That's a positive comment. So, fine. So. We have one ... sort of ... civil exchange. Let's try for more. Mom? Tell us what you've been doing.

EVELYN. Me? Oh — nothing. You know me.

KESS. What'd you do this morning?

EVELYN. Went out for a walk.

KESS. And?

EVELYN. I walked.

KESS. Did you see anybody?

EVELYN. Certainly.

KESS. *(A beat.)* Who?

EVELYN. Who? Um ... Mrs. Matthews.

KESS. How was she?

EVELYN. Fine. I didn't really have a very eventful morning. Why don't we go to Jo?

KESS. Did you and Mrs. Matthews talk?

EVELYN. Yes, but...

KESS. What about?

EVELYN. Oh, nothing much.

KESS. What?

EVELYN. Just ... Jo.

KESS. Jo. Fine. Did she have anything nice to say about Jo?

EVELYN. Of course. She's always liked Jo. Why don't we talk about...?

KESS. What exactly did she say about Jo?

EVELYN. Nothing. Just that Jo's a very strong girl in some ways.

KESS. Did you hear that, Jo? Now, that's exactly what I mean, Mom. Why should you be slow to tell us a thing like that?

EVELYN. Well...

KESS. What's strong about her? How did it come up?

EVELYN. Oh, I don't know...

KESS. It must've come from something.

EVELYN. Not really.

KESS. Mom, what aren't you telling us?

EVELYN. Nothing.

JO. Mom? What is it?

EVELYN. Oh, Jo — I'll tell you later, all right? When we're alone.

JO. Is it private?

EVELYN. Well...

SHERRY. So what is it? Don getting married or something?

EVELYN. Who told you?

SHERRY. You're kidding. That was a joke.

JO. Don's getting married?

KESS. Mom, what are you...?

JO. Who to?

EVELYN. I was going to tell you later...

JO. *Who to?!*

EVELYN. Heidi Joy Duckly. Mrs. Matthews heard it this morning from Heidi's mother.

JO. Oh, God...

KESS. Jo...

JO. Oh, *God.*

KESS. Jo, listen — there are two ways to handle this.

SHERRY. Yeah? Suicide and what?

KESS. Shut up!

SHERRY. Very positive.

KESS. Jo, we can fly off the handle here, or we can be calm about it. We can find something useful in it.

JO. *Useful?!*

KESS. Yes. Something. That's the problem with us. Trouble comes, and we break down. Let's not do that.

SHERRY. Heidi's folks must feel great to get rid of her. The wedding oughta be a prize pork show.

KESS. *Sherry.*

SHERRY. She's only losing a Subaru.

EVELYN. I think you're lucky to be rid of him.

JO. I'm not *lucky! (She rises, moves toward the stairs.)*

KESS. Where are you going?

JO. My room! *(But she stops suddenly, slumps against the archway.)*

SHERRY. What are you stopping for?

JO. We used to make love up there.

EVELYN. That's the trouble with an old house. It always fills up with ghosts. Good memories turn into bad ones. I know I see your father in every room. Not literally, of course. Speaking of memories, Jo — do you know what I've been doing in the attic?

JO. What?

EVELYN. I've been painting. Just a little, every day. Guess what I've been painting.

JO. What?

EVELYN. The baby furniture. All the baby furniture — yours and Kess's and Sherry's. I've been making it new for your new baby. I was going to keep it a secret, but I think you can use a little good news right now. Would you like to come up and see?

JO. Well..

EVELYN. Oh, come on. It's turning out so nice. Your baby is going to live right here with us — with her mother and her grandma. Just the way I did when I was a little girl. And she's going to be every bit as happy and well-cared-for and loved as I was. Doesn't that sound nice? Wouldn't you like to come up and see?

JO. All right.

KESS. Jo...

EVELYN. *(Rising.)* Good.

KESS. Jo — don't you think it would be better to keep trying this? You can see the furniture later.

JO. *(A beat.)* I'm going up. *(Jo turns and hurries upstairs.)*

KESS. Jo...!

EVELYN. Kess, I'm sorry this game didn't work out. Maybe we'll do better another time. *(Evelyn exits upstairs.)*

KESS. *(A beat.)* You see what I'm trying to do, don't you?

SHERRY. Sure. You're trying to make a family where there isn't one. *(A beat.)* Jo and I are going to see the new James Bond tonight. Want to come? *(A beat.)* Be a chance to get away from Mom.

KESS. *(A beat.)* All right.

54

SHERRY. Good. *(Sherry exits into her room. Kess sighs, leans her head back on the couch. Her hand moves up to touch the cameo. Lights slowly fade to black.)*

Scene Three

Late that same night. The room is empty, the tea set is gone. After a moment, we hear the giggling of Kess, Jo and Sherry outside the porch.

SHERRY. *(Off.)* I'm not going in first. Jo, you go.

JO. *(Off.)* Why don't you?

SHERRY. *(Off.)* Kess?

KESS. *(Off.)* You're standing next to the door. Go on in.

SHERRY. *(Off.)* What if Mom's in there?

KESS. *(Off.)* Of course she's in there...

SHERRY. *(Off.)* But what if she's waiting for us? With a plate?

KESS and JO. *(Off, disapprovingly.)* Sherry...

SHERRY. *(Entering.)* Ok, ok. Lousy joke.

JO. *(Entering with Kess.)* Very lousy.

KESS. Mom? We're back. Mom? *(Looking into the kitchen.)* Where are you?

JO. I'll go look in her room. *(Jo exits upstairs.)*

KESS. You think we made enough noise walking home?

SHERRY. I still say we should've hit Popeye's for a beer.

KESS. Jo's pregnant.

SHERRY. *I'm* not.

KESS. It's been a long time since I actually enjoyed walking around this town. Maybe I should make some coffee.

SHERRY. What is this thing between you and caffeine? *(Jo reenters.)*

JO. She's ok.

55

SHERRY. She's ok and I'm sober. *(Flops into a chair.)*
KESS. I'm glad we did this tonight. We saw a good movie.
JO. You think so? I didn't like it.
SHERRY. You're just mad 'cause the woman didn't die.
JO. I think that really changes things...
SHERRY. Sure. Dead, you don't mind. What you hate is when they sail off into the sunset for a lifetime of meaningless sex.
JO. Well, yes, as a matter of fact.
SHERRY. Believe me, big sister — it's the best way to get out of this house. Dedicate yourself to meaningless sex.
JO. Don't be ridiculous.
SHERRY. I mean it. You should go out and do it with whoever you want, whenever you feel like it, and not think about it afterwards. Puts you in a very different state of mind.
JO. I can't do that.
SHERRY. Sure you can. Want me to set you up? I know a bunch of guys — we'll toss their names in a hat. It's what I do myself.
KESS. How many lovers have you had?
SHERRY. My share. And all meaningless, too. I'm the first lady of meaningless sex. You guys screw up 'cause you think it's supposed to mean something.
JO. It does.
SHERRY. No, it doesn't. I slept with a guy once 'cause I liked his socks. What'd that mean?
KESS. Not much, I guess.
SHERRY. Damn right. I've slept with guys who would make you vomit. This one I knew was really sloppy. A total pig. But I wondered if maybe he was just profound and didn't have time for cleaning. So I went home with him.
KESS. Naturally.
SHERRY. His place was incredible. It looked like he cooked in the bedroom and slept in the kitchen. So anyway — we did it on this bare mattress on the floor. And when we got done, he rolled over, reached under the dresser, among all the hairballs and shit, and pulled out a spoon.

JO. Oh, God! God! Stop it!

SHERRY. And he said, "Want some chili?"

JO. Sherry, stop it! Ew!

SHERRY. Hey — truth is gross.

JO. Well, I've never had any meaningless sex.

SHERRY. Ever faked an orgasm?

KESS. I faked an orgasm with a woman. *(They look at her.)* I mean, if you want to talk meaningless.

SHERRY. You're kidding.

KESS. If you want to talk true meaningless, I've had sex with a man, just so I could meet his sister. Top that.

SHERRY. You really did that?

KESS. Yes, when I was young and stupid.

SHERRY. I had sex with a guy at a concert and never even knew his name. Top that.

JO. You guys...

KESS. I had sex with a woman in a dorm laundry, and never even saw her face.

SHERRY. Yeah, but did you talk to her? I never talked to my guy at the concert.

JO. You guys! Is this all we can talk about? I don't care what either of you did. I think it's more disgusting to talk about that kind of sex than to have it.

SHERRY. I'd rather be disgusting than pitiful. You've got the most screwed-up sex life I ever...

JO. *I'm* screwed? You're the one who always forgets who she had the night before.

SHERRY. At least I have someone to forget.

JO. I had someone.

SHERRY. Yeah, and now he's marrying Heidi. Hope you and Mom'll be very happy together.

JO. *(A beat. Quietly.)* Well, at least with Don it wasn't meaningless.

SHERRY. Oh, yes it was.

KESS. Why don't we talk about the movie?

SHERRY. It was. Simpleton thinks Don was faithful the whole

time they were together.

JO. He was faithful.

SHERRY. Don slept with at least six girls while you were dating. Including Heidi.

JO. How do you know that?

SHERRY. They told me.

JO. You're lying! That's just a complete lie.

SHERRY. Wake up. Don sleeps with everybody in town.

KESS. You guys...

JO. He does not!

SHERRY. Oh yeah? He slept with me! *(A beat. They are all perfectly still.)* Once.

JO. When? *(A beat.)* When?!

SHERRY. After you dropped him. What do you care? It's all meaningless.

JO. Not to me!

SHERRY. For God's sake, Heidi's the one who should be mad, not you. I wouldn't've told you, but you just keep being so pitiful about it all. You want him and then you don't want him... *(She trails off, in deep embarrassment.)* I'm sorry.

JO. It's so easy for us to criticize Mom. To say she made us like we are. But she never did anything just for the cruelty of it. If she hurts us, it's because she's afraid, and disappointed and doesn't want to be left alone. But we do it just for the fun.

KESS. Jo...

JO. We're supposed to be the healthy ones. Aren't we? Aren't we? *(She rises.)* Good night. *(Jo exits in silence. Kess looks at Sherry.)*

SHERRY. I'm sorry. It slipped out. *(A beat.)* Maybe we should have some coffee.

KESS. As long as you make it on your knees.

SHERRY. *(Exiting into the kitchen.)* I said I was sorry. *(Kess starts for the stairs, stops. Sherry calls from the kitchen.)* Hey, what are these letters on the counter?

KESS. The mail. I brought it in today.

SHERRY. *(Off.)* No wonder I can never find it. *(A beat.)* Hey! Hey, Kess! I got a letter! From Spinner!

58

KESS. Spinner?

SHERRY. *(Off.)* My biker!

KESS. Oh. Wonderful.

SHERRY. *(Reentering with the letter.)* No, Kess — wait! It's from a *gallery!!* He enclosed a letter from a gallery! It's the ... um, the Raoul Gallery in ... um, *BROOKLYN!!* They want to talk to *me!*

KESS. About what?

SHERRY. About me, about my work! Don't you see? Spinner really took my stuff to New York! I didn't think he would, but he did! And they love my slides! They're calling my stuff a whole new school of art! It's ... it's ... um, Post-Post-Modern Infantilist! Isn't that great!? I'm knocking 'em dead back there!

KESS. Sherry...

SHERRY. Kess! They want to do a show! They want me there right now! Just when I was starting to think he didn't really work for Walt Disney!

KESS. They want you where?

SHERRY. New York! For the show. They want to fly me in. Do you know how they live in New York? They are total animals! I can't *wait!* I'm flying tomorrow.

KESS. Who pays?

SHERRY. What?

KESS. Who buys the plane ticket?

SHERRY. I do. Why not? The whole point is getting the chance.

KESS. What's the name of the gallery?

SHERRY. The Raoul Gallery.

KESS. Sherry.

SHERRY. What?

KESS. The *Raoul* Gallery? In Brooklyn?

SHERRY. What's wrong with that?

KESS. It's ridiculous. It's a joke.

SHERRY. You think they're not real?

KESS. Sherry...

SHERRY. *(Defensively.)* They're real. They've got a letterhead. They're real.

KESS. Sure.

SHERRY. They're real!

KESS. Can't you see that Spinner is just doing this to you? God knows why, but...

SHERRY. Spinner is a professional!

KESS. A professional what — that's the question.

SHERRY. Spinner and I had the one honest exchange of my whole senior year.

KESS. How much did you exchange?

SHERRY. Damn it, if he says it's real, then it's real!

KESS. Sherry, look at me. Come on, look in my face. Do you really believe there is a Post-Post-Modern Infantilist school of art?

SHERRY. *(Exploding.) Yes!!* God damn it! I believe more in that than in this goddamn, stupid fucking family! There *is* a Raoul Gallery!

KESS. Sherry...

SHERRY. There is!

KESS. Sherry, take it easy...

SHERRY. I'm having a show! And I'm going!

KESS. *(Touching her.)* Shh — I know you are.

SHERRY. I am!

KESS. I know, it's all right.

SHERRY. It's in Brooklyn! *(She is near tears.)*

KESS. *(Taking hold of her.)* I know. I know it is.

SHERRY. Brooklyn, New York. And I'm going, I'm...

KESS. Shh. I know. You're going to New York. I know. You're going to New York. *(They are silent. Kess holds her and rocks her.)*

SHERRY. *(Quietly.)* How did Mom live a whole life here?

KESS. She had us. *(Lights slowly fade to black.)*

Scene Four

Afternoon, the next day. No one is onstage. Jo rushes in the front door.

JO. Kess? Kess!?

KESS. *(Off.)* I'm upstairs!

JO. Can you come down?

KESS. *(Off.)* In a minute. *(Jo looks around the room, goes to Sherry's door, looks in.)*

JO. Sherry? You home? *(No response. Jo stands nervously.)* Kess!

KESS. *(Off.)* I'm coming, I'm coming! *(Kess enters from upstairs.)* What's wrong?

JO. Where were you?

KESS. Upstairs.

JO. Nobody seemed to be here.

KESS. What's wrong?

JO. Where's Mom?

KESS. She's at the store.

JO. Where's Sherry?

KESS. With Mom. Jo, what are you...?

JO. So, they're not here.

KESS. *(A beat.)* Jo, where have you been all morning?

JO. On an errand.

KESS. A four-hour errand?

JO. I had to go over to Waterloo. *(A beat.)* Kess, do you remember when you asked me to come up and stay with you?

KESS. Yes.

JO. Did you mean that?

KESS. Well ... yes, at the time...

JO. I want to come up. I want to come up right now.

KESS. Now?

61

JO. Yes. And I want to stay. I want to stay for the summer at least, maybe a lot longer.

KESS. Jo, what are you talking about?

JO. I want to come up. You said I could come up. You said that roommate of yours, that...

KESS. Susan.

JO. You said Susan thinks it's ok.

KESS. Well, yes, but ... why now?

JO. I have to get away from Mom.

KESS. What'd she do?

JO. Nothing.

KESS. *(A beat.)* Yesterday you and Mom were planning which room to use for the nursery. What happened? Why are you so scared?

JO. I just did a ... very odd thing. I went over to Heidi's house. I thought I was only going over to talk with her. Just to ... look her in the eye once, and ask her if she really slept with Don while he and I were ... you know, like Sherry said...

KESS. I know.

JO. But as I turned the corner I saw her pull out and drive away. So I followed her.

KESS. To Waterloo? *(Jo nods.)* What did you do there?

JO. I watched. I watched the way she drove. I watched the way she shopped. She hit all the bridal shops, plus a few others. She's a good shopper.

KESS. Did she see you?

JO. No. I hid. I stayed two cars behind her, like on tv, and I hid behind pillars in the stores. I never lost her. I stared at her and stared at her for four hours, and she never saw me and I never lost her. I didn't want to talk with her anymore. I just wanted to watch her. On the way home, I thought, "My God, why am I doing this!?" But I just kept following. I thought, "*Mom* should be driving this car. I should be Mom doing this." Then I thought, "I am." Kess, I love Mom.

KESS. I know that.

JO. I thought of how I'll be in ten years, if I stay with Mom. Kess, I can't be Mom. How can I help her if I'm just like her?

KESS. Jo...

JO. I want to leave tomorrow. And I want to stay with you. Is that all right?

KESS. Well ... I'm not sure that's the best idea anymore.

JO. *Kess...*

KESS. Jo, we can't leave Mom the way she is. I thought we could, but that was before I saw how lonely she was...

JO. I don't care...

KESS. Besides, she could hurt herself. That's why I've stayed down here so long — to make sure she's all right.

JO. She's all right; let's go.

KESS. She's not all right.

JO. She never will be!

KESS. Jo, what if I stay down here another few days, and then come back on regular visits, once a month, for as long as ... for as long as it takes? Could you stay here then?

JO. No! I'm coming up north, and I'm living with you. You offered it. And I need it.

KESS. Jo...

JO. You owe me! *(A beat.)* I don't care how guilty you feel, Kess. I don't. We can't save Mom. Save me. *(We suddenly hear Sherry and Evelyn at the front door.)*

SHERRY. Here we are — Shopper's Anonymous. *(Entering.)* Hi, everybody. It's everybody else. Where'd you go this morning, Jo? Somewhere fun?

JO. No.

SHERRY. *(Carrying the bag into the kitchen.)* Should've come with us. The store was full of living sculptures.

EVELYN. *(At the screen door, with a bag of groceries.)* Can someone help me with the door?

KESS. *(Hurrying to open it.)* Oh — sorry.

EVELYN. Thank you. Hi, Jo. Did you have a good morning? Oh, let me set these *down. (Doing so, on the couch.)* There. Why is modern food so heavy? Sherry and I decided to have a big dinner tonight, for Kess. We haven't really done that yet, and Kess is starting to fit in so well.

SHERRY. *(Reentering, to Kess)* Yeah. Are you sure you're not crazy?

EVELYN. Jo, do you want to help me cook it?

JO. No.

EVELYN. Oh? Are you busy tonight?

JO. No.

EVELYN. *(A beat.)* Oh. Well, maybe you can, Kess.

JO. She can't either.

EVELYN. Why not?

KESS. Jo, this isn't the right time...

JO. She'll be packing. So will I.

EVELYN. Packing? What for?

JO. I'm going to Minneapolis with her.

EVELYN. *(A beat.)* Really?

JO. Yes.

EVELYN. I don't understand. You mean for a visit?

JO. No.

EVELYN. For longer?

JO. Forever.

EVELYN. *(A beat.)* You're pregnant. You can't travel.

JO. Two and a half months. We're not going by covered wagon.

KESS. Jo...

EVELYN. Oh, this is a joke. Isn't it? You and Kess have created a joke. Oh, I see now. Well, it's very funny. *(She takes an orange out of the bag.)* Isn't this a joke, Kess?

KESS. No, not exactly...

JO. Mom, I've been following Heidi around.

EVELYN. Following Heidi? What for?

JO. Just to watch her. Just to watch what she does all day.

SHERRY. That must be a thrill.

JO. I couldn't help myself. I just followed her.

EVELYN. We all have impulses that are hard to control. *(She tosses the orange casually onto the couch.)*

JO. I'm afraid I'll go crazy.

EVELYN. *(Flaring.)* What in hell do you know about it?! I've *been* in mental hospitals!

JO. I was only...

EVELYN. You were only trying to sneak out of here! In the dust of everybody else galloping away! *(She tosses another orange onto the couch.)*

SHERRY. Mom, what are you doing?

EVELYN. What?

SHERRY. You're putting oranges on the couch.

EVELYN. Well, of course I'm putting oranges on the couch! This is my house. People used to live in it. *(A beat.)* Who's going to stay here?

JO. Well ... Sherry...

EVELYN. She'll be out the door twenty seconds after commencement.

JO. Kess says she'll visit...

EVELYN. Who'll *live* here?

JO. When I followed Heidi, I even followed her home. I did. I sat in my car and watched her mother come out and help her bring in the things she'd bought. They were laughing. They looked like sisters.

EVELYN. Jo...

JO. You're crazy! And when you're not crazy, you're angry. When you're not angry, you're demanding. It can be months between times we have any pleasure!

EVELYN. Jo...

JO. I'm the only person who has ever put up with you!

EVELYN. *(Reaching to embrace her.)* Jo...

JO. *(Retreating.)* No! I'm living with Kess. I have to. I have to.

EVELYN. *(A beat.)* You can't. You can't, and that's all there is to it. It's a ridiculous idea. Kess, was this your idea?

KESS. No...

EVELYN. Jo could never live with you. She's going to have a baby.

KESS. What are you talking about?

EVELYN. You could never live with a baby.

KESS. Of course I could live with a baby.

EVELYN. You don't know the first thing. You'd panic in a minute.

KESS. I can live with a baby!

EVELYN. *You don't know what they want!*

JO. It's my baby!

EVELYN. You shut up! I'm talking to Kess.

KESS. Mom, what if Jo just comes up for a little while? Just to see how it goes?

JO. *No.*

KESS. We could come down on visits.

JO. *No!*

EVELYN. Do you really want to take her from me?

JO. I'm going!

KESS. I don't want to take anybody from anybody...

EVELYN. Well, that's what you're doing. You girls would like a world full of strangers, wouldn't you? You'd like it if there was no connection between people at all. *(Focussing on Jo.)* Well, there isn't. Not unless you make one. Kess and Henry taught me that. They were the two most silent people I ever knew. For eight years they were my whole family. Henry and Kess. Can you imagine what dinners were like? I had to beg Henry for you. You were all I ever got out of my whole family. You're the only one I can look at and not see Henry.

JO. *(Backing away.)* I can't help you.

EVELYN. Then who can?

JO. I can't help you.

EVELYN. I just need you to be here a little more. Just a few days.

JO. I can't! I can't help you, I can't be with you, I can't look at you, I can't think about you, I can't talk to you, I can't hope for you...

EVELYN. Can you love me?

JO. *It's not a matter of love!!*

EVELYN. Can you?

JO. Kess!

EVELYN. What do you think families are for? Do you think parents die when you turn 21? I might as well have, if all you're leaving me is the Mental Health Institute and a townful of people saying, "Poor Evelyn Briggs. First her husband walks off, then every one of her daughters abandons her."

KESS. We're not abandoning you. We'll be back. We'll visit.

EVELYN. When? How often?

KESS. Once a month.

EVELYN. Once a month?

KESS. Twice, then. Twice a month.

JO. No...!

KESS. *Jo!* Mom? What do you say?

EVELYN. I have wasted my life raising three *animals!!*

JO. *(To Kess.)* I won't come down!

EVELYN. I lived my life for you! My mother lived her life for me. That's what family means — each generation destroying itself willingly, for what comes after. Even if it's you! *(A silence. Kess slowly unpins the cameo from her dress.)*

KESS. *(Quietly.)* Jo and I are going to go upstairs and pack. We'll talk about visits later. *(Placing the cameo on a table next to Evelyn.)* I think you should keep this for awhile. *(A beat. Kess starts for the stairs.)* Come on, Jo. *(As Jo starts after her, Evelyn reaches into the grocery bag and pulls out a can. She raises it high in the air.)*

SHERRY. Mom! *(Evelyn smashes the can down on the cameo.)*

JO. *NO!*

KESS. Mom!

SHERRY. Jesus! *(A beat. The heirloom is in pieces.)*

JO. How could you do that? How could you do that?!

EVELYN. Because it was mine. *(Lights fade to black.)*

Scene Five

Morning, the next day. Before lights rise we hear Sherry's voice in the darkness. Lights slowly fade up midway through her song to reveal her sitting with Kess's ballad book open in her lap.

SHERRY.
"Tis down in yonder garden green,
Love where we used to walk,
The finest flower that e'er was seen
Is withered to a stalk.
(She shifts from the traditional tune to a punk version.)
The stalk is withered dry, my love
So will our hearts decay..."
(Kess enters through the porch, and Sherry immediately snaps the book shut.)
KESS. Is Jo ready? I've got all my stuff in the car.
SHERRY. *(Holding the book up.)* You don't have this.
KESS. *(Taking it.)* Oh — thanks. Jo upstairs?
SHERRY. Guess so.
KESS. What'll you do? When we're gone?
SHERRY. Graduate. Move out.
KESS. *(A beat.)* You're welcome to come and see us, if you ever...
SHERRY. *(Suddenly rising.)* Look, I'm going to go over to Ed Randall's for awhile. If Mom asks, tell her I'm there, ok?
KESS. Sure... Don't you want to say goodby to Jo?
SHERRY. No, that's ok.
KESS. Sherry?
SHERRY. What?
KESS. Glad I got to know you again.
SHERRY. Yeah, well... see you in four years. *(Sherry exits out the front. Kess looks around the room a little nervously, then calls.)*
KESS. Jo-o! I'm all set! *(Jo enters from upstairs with a pair of bags.)*
JO. Here I am.
KESS. Is that all your stuff?
JO. The rest is in the car.

KESS. Well ... then, um ... let's go, I guess.

JO. Could you take these out? I'd like to say goodby to Mom.

KESS. I already tried. It's not much use.

JO. Could you anyway? *(Kess shrugs, takes the bags.)*

KESS. I'll be in the car. *(Kess exits out the front.)*

JO. *(Calling upstairs.)* Mom?! I'm leaving! Mom? Could you come down? *(Jo waits uncomfortably for a moment.)* Mom?! *(She waits again. Finally she shakes her head and starts for the front door. Evelyn appears from upstairs.)* Oh — um, we're leaving now.

EVELYN. I know.

JO. I'm sorry I took so long to pack. *(A beat.)* I'm going to write, you know. Whether or not you write back. *(A beat.)* And ... I will visit, after awhile. If you'd like me to. *(A beat.)* I talked to Mrs. Anderberg. She said she'll be glad to come over, as much as you need.

EVELYN. That's nice. She wasn't really born here, you know. She's from Michigan.

JO. I called Dr. Hanson. He'd like to talk with you sometime. Just talk. Whenever you'd like to.

EVELYN. *(A beat.)* Is there anything else?

JO. I want to hug you.

EVELYN. *(A beat.)* Go ahead. Hug me. *(Jo hesitates, then does so. Evelyn doesn't resist, but neither does she raise her arms to hug back. Jo steps back and stares at her.)*

JO. I could call when we get up there. This afternoon, I mean. *(A beat.)* I think I will. *(A beat. Jo starts to leave, stops.)* Should I? *(A beat. Jo leaves. Lights slowly fade to black as Evelyn remains still.)*

THE END

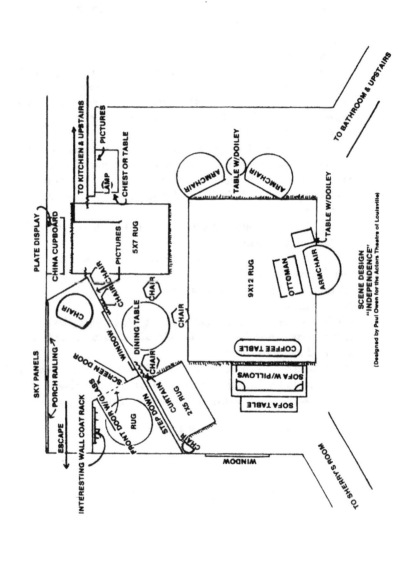

SCENE DESIGN
"INDEPENDENCE"
(Designed by Paul Owen for the Actors Theatre of Louisville)

PROPERTY LIST

ACT ONE

Scene One
Couch
Overstuffed chairs
Three framed photographs (preset on table)
Orthopedic collar
Travel bag
Mirror
Makeup kit
Brush
Hair (pulled from brush)
Clothes (in travel bag)
Hardcover book (in travel bag)
Table

Scene Two
Hardcover book (same as in Scene One)
Paperback book
Two cups
Hostess cupcake

Scene Three
Dustpan with broken glass
Broom
Damaged photograph
Magazine
Cameo

Scene Four
Pile of slides
Paperback baby-name book
Towel

Scene One
Scrabble game
Score pad
Pencil
Scissors

Scene Two
Tea for four
Tray

Scene Three
Letter

Scene Four
Two bags of groceries
Two oranges
A can

Scene Five
Book from Act One, Scene One
Two travel bags